THE JOURNEY OF AN
IMPATIENT SOUL

Anupam Chakrabarti

INDIA • SINGAPORE • MALAYSIA

ISBN 979-8-89777-673-3

Dedicated to my Gurudeva

Shree Guru Vishwamitra

With the blessings of

Lord Shiva

Mata Parvati

And

Shree Ganesha

PREFACE

This book is meant to be read with an open mind. Whatever is written may seem fanciful. But I have been ordered by my Gurudeva to communicate such data and visions, and I will write only the truth. So that truth is not distorted, I am writing these myself. If your feelings are hurt, I apologize. I am not asking anybody to believe in anything. I strongly believe in science and I would try my best to keep my writings to the point and as scientific as possible. However, few things are indeed, beyond science.

Dated: 27th January, 2025   Anupam Chakrabarti

Kolkata, West Bengal, India.

INDEX

Chapter 1:

HOW TO CHOOSE YOUR GURU

You may be deeply religious and even understand that there is a path to God. But you are like a driverless car riding on a highway. There is no surety where you will end up. Life has got a limited time, and every life requires a different path to the Creator. This is precisely why almost all of us require a Guru.

How to choose a Guru?

I will highlight the important requirements:

- Significantly better than you in all respects.

- Proven credentials – must have Shishyas or pupils who have achieved their goals.

- A Guru is just like your father. You should be fully comfortable to completely surrender to him. His place will be at par to God. For you, he will be the manifested God on earth.

Mostly you will find many Gurus searching for disciples for money or fame. True ones are not found easily. Simply because these elevated souls can see beyond the maya or illusion of the society. They are not interested in your body, money, power, fame, etc. If you are really bent on finding, you will actually come to realize that your Guru has already been destined for you. And if you can't seek him out, he will!

Once you feel he is the one, test him if you want. A true Guru would love to be tested. Tell him that you have left your home and family, you have no money, you are a nobody but a vagabond, and see his reaction. There are other subtle ways of testing him, can try them out. Anyway, once you are done, now the real Guru will test you to see and understand whether you are a capable student, and how capable you are. He will test you in whatever way he wants to build you up. If only you pass the tests, will he accept you as a Shishya (pupil).

Never expect an instant Deeksha (initiation to a mantra). You need to persevere for years to get that. In the meantime, both you and your Guru will know all about each other. There will be a mutual respect and a tremendous bond which will transcend lives.

When you realize the time has come, your Guru will realize it too, and you will get your Mantra Deeksha. However, not everyone requires or is entitled to such. Your Guru will remain the best person how to guide your life. As each person is unique, so is each Shishya. You will get your personalized Deeksha, which can be extremely different from your best friend from the same Guru.

Chapter 2:
THE CONCEPT OF THE CREATOR

Let us say, I assembled three computers, and started using them connecting them to the internet. Let us call them A, B and C. Let us see what the created think or understand about the Creator.

A thought that the Creator has an eye so that he could see. He can listen because he uses speakers. Since he can type, he must have a hand with a few fingers.

B said he agrees with all that A understood about the Creator. But he also uses sites regarding religion and religious studies, and also sites related to science, biology and medicine. B deduced he must be an old man with an eye, hearing abilities, and possibly a healer.

My daughter was using C. C disagreed with them on multiple points. C said the Creator is young and has at least 4 or 10 hands with many fingers as he could type very fast. The Creator is a young female, as she regularly plays computer games and is interested in all sorts of girlish videos. She also has 2 ears as she uses headphones. She can talk with a mike.

Now, A, B and C come together and confer about their concepts of the Creator. A said the Creator had one eye, one hand, a few fingers, is an elderly man, has hearing ability. B agreed and added that he might have been a healer by profession. Now, C countered both of them. C said the Creator was a young female, who had one eye, two ears, multiple hands and plenty of fingers, who can speak.

You can make any number of such combinations and inferences. I have taken this only as a sort of example.

So, the created will always be a confused lot. No creature can fully understand the Creator unless He wants you to. There is no use arguing whether there is one Creator or many, has one hand or many, has one eye or a thousand etc. because these arguments are base and never ending.

The Divine knowledge of the Creator and the Creation is called Brahmagyan. The only way to achieve it is to surrender yourself completely to Him. Be immersed in Karmayog, as has been described in the Geeta. Do your work without the thought of awards or rewards. A reward should be equal to a punishment. So why do any work? So along with Karmayog, one needs to start a disciplined life, meditate on the Lord, thank Him for whatever He has given and also start on the process of Sankhayog, a state of ultimate learnedness, where you know that doing something or not won't affect anything. Sankhayog is much more difficult to achieve, and can only be achieved after you have been a Karmayogi for years or decades.

The ultimate aim of our Atma is to identify Self with the Parameshwara. Once you achieve that, you are free from the cycle of birth and death. The liberated soul will be one with the Lord and attain a state of permanent bliss. This is the ultimate achievement of each one of us, have no doubt on that. Whether you are a plant, a bird, an insect, a lion, or a human, each soul will strive through many lives to attain this permanent bliss.

What role should a scripture play? Every scripture shows you how an elevated soul journeyed through life to get further elevation or liberation. All of them are correct in their own way that they show you a path. But each individual is different. And each one must seek his own path for elevation or liberation.

All beings must be seekers. Seekers of the Ultimate. Read scriptures, keep your mind open, believe what your logical mind allows you to believe, and don't believe what you don't want to. Never be dogmatic. The worst mistake that people nowadays do, is extreme dogmatism. They are firm believers of what somebody else sought. What somebody can seek is only a very small fraction of the Ultimate! Once you firmly believe in somebody else's seek and his life's achievement, you close your mind's eye and box yourself into a corner. Open your mind!

Chapter 3:

MY CONCEPT OF THE CREATOR

Whatever little I have understood of this Creation, if you believe there is one Creator, it must be a female energy. Without a female energy, there cannot be Creation or sustenance. But I have always felt this Creation is an interplay between female and male energies, because they are complimentary. One may ask, does the Creator have a form? Can we communicate with Him?

I have never seen a form, but some have. So I don't rule out that He or She could have a form. Till date, I have only seen intense and brilliant light in my meditation, so brilliant that you can hardly see through or concentrate what's behind. I have occasionally seen fire as well, sometimes durba (sacred grass), bel patra, symbol of OM, trishul, but never any form.

I have seen a few forms which appeared extraordinary. First, in 2013, in Srisailam, after doing a Rudrabhishek I was returning to my hotel with my mother-in-law, I encountered two similar looking males, young in their 20s, clad in white, at least six feet or more in height, looking great, speaking fluent English, wearing very bright white shirts and pants, asked me for some food, saying, they didn't take food for the last two days. All of this happening in fluent English, as I am a Bengali and Srisailam is in Andhra. I wasn't carrying any money as it is not allowed to carry moneybag, mobile, etc in the Mandir. I turned to my mother-in-law and asked her to give them some money, she went in the hotel, I turned round to face them, found they were gone!!

I visited Haridwar with my family sometime in May, 2014, and after visiting a very old Mahadev mandir, my family was already seated in an auto, I saw a very graceful male saint, clad in new or very clean saffron clothes, having not a single white hair in his moustache or beard or head, and yet glowing with Gyan (knowledge) . I had an uncanny habit of guessing the age of any person I met since 1995, my third year MBBS, when we were taught to guess the apparent age of the patient and match it with the actual age. I had practised it on everyone I met since, and I could guess an age within 2 or 3 years in most cases. I looked hard at him, straight in his eyes and tried very hard to guess his age. Such knowledge was not compatible with the age coming to my mind, and I couldn't come to a number. Meanwhile, he glanced at me twice from foot to head, and then straight at my eyes without blinking. Must have been a minute or two, when both of us were looking hard at each other's eyes without blinking with me trying hard to calculate his age in my mind. Then I thought, after all, he is a sanyasi, not my patient. I smiled, bowed down, folded my hand in pranam, took out my wallet, saw two notes, one of ten, the other of hundred, thought that I would require the hundred to pay the auto and gave him the ten. He extended his hand, accepted the note, turned back and went in the Mandir, not a word exchanged. I could understand he was out of the ordinary. I thought about the sage Markandeya, who was always young, then Lord Parashuram, my Gurudev, but didn't understand who he was. Many years later, during the yearly Kali puja, I recounted the story to my family priest. He instantly told me he was my Lord, who is ageless. I had been practising the Tatpurusha gayatri since at least one year then, must have appeared in the Tatpurusha form. I was dismayed and stunned, thinking why I didn't give everything I had to Him! How could the Lord Himself come to me so quickly, when so many can't achieve Him after years? And how could I not think about Him but almost everyone else? But that's how special encounters happen. You will only know that you are encountering the Lord Himself, only if He wants to!

The third incident also happened in 2015 or so. I was walking to my chamber when out of nowhere came in front of me a young boy in his twenties, with a long shikha and visible janeu, wearing a dhoti and a cloth covering part of his upper body, holding a kamandalu, full of energy, almost jumping up and down. He asked me who was my Ishtadevata, I was about to answer, suddenly I thought why should I communicate my secrets with unknown people. And I told him, I worship everybody. I was wearing three golden rings with a diamond, a ruby and a pearl.

He got hold of my right index finger and tried very hard to get the pearl ring out into his kamandalu. However, it was too tight to take out. He kept on trying for an inordinate time, while I kept telling him, it won't come out because it was too tight. He didn't try the other two gold rings which would have come out easily. As I was getting late, I offered him a 50 rupee note, and went on my way. I thought he may have been Hanumanjee or Naradjee.

The most interesting part is that in all these cases, other people either didn't see them, or don't remember them at all, while even after so many years, I remember everything very distinctly.

Can you communicate with the Nirakara or the Divine Light?

The answer is Yes! Once you start having the small glowing circle of light in darkness during meditation, you will start to communicate with the Divine.

The light is intense. Jyotiswaroopa Nirakara. Will He answer all your questions? No, but He will choose to answer most. Because most of our questions are base. You get an answer almost immediately. What language does He understand? He is a mind reader – don't worry about your language! What about people who believe in many Gods? Worship idols? Worship the Sun/ Fire? Let everyone believe in God in whatever form they feel comfortable. Not everyone can sense or worship God in the Nirakara or the Formless One. People often need symbolism. How do you worship the Lord?

What I have felt, according to decreasing order of effectiveness:

- Tapas: intense meditation after renouncing the world.

- Meditation: daily meditation on the Nirakara or whatever you like or love.

- Japa: repeated chanting of a well -recognized mantra, whether you understand the meaning or not. Repeated chanting hits your brain, and over years, it works.

- Pitru tarpana: daily offering water with black sesame seeds, which opens the door of Vaikuntha or Heaven for them. Their blessings enhance your luck and often breaks barriers of luck beyond human capabilities.

- Offering water to the Sun: daily in the morning, first word you speak is worship the Sun, without whom there would be no life at all, and offer some water.

- Havan: daily or weekly doing at least a small fire sacrifice.

- Vrata or fasting.

- Yoga and keeping fit. Taking good care of your physical body is very important, because the soul can work its way only when you are not disturbed by ill health, physically or mentally.

Does bhajan, keertan, songs in praise of the Lord help? They do. But difficult for me to place it in this order.

How effective are the Scriptures? They tell us about the observations and experiences of great saints. Experience of someone else in attaining God. Problem is that none of the scriptures have been written by they themselves. So all of them have been corrupted or edited slowly but surely over the years.

It is thus important to keep the mind clear and not be obstinate. Be a seeker. Often the stepping stones are the small rituals like keeping a fast on a particular day of the week, visiting the Mosque on Fridays or the Church on Sundays, giving alms, donating food, etc. While symbolic, they will slowly draw you to spirituality and to the realization of Self or the Nirakara. Don't ridicule someone not following your path. The path to the Formless One is quite complicated and it will require years of soul searching and introspection.

Once you have realized the Formless One, you will find Him in the specks of dust and space as well. Then the rituals will have no meaning for you. But they will still act as stepping stones for the others. Encourage others to attain this blissful state as well rather than saying, Ah! These are of no use!

Chapter 4:
YOUR GOD ON EARTH

Your father, mother and teachers are the first Gurus that all of us encounter. Till the time your mother and father remain alive, they will always be your God on earth. Even if your parents are not as you would have liked them to be, know it to be your destiny that you have received these people as your parents. There are a few things in life over which you have no control. Shouldn't complain about them. Accept them as your destiny. The status of the mother is the highest, since she has taken all the pains to carry you for 9 months and then fed you.

Next is your father. It is because of him that you were born. This man mostly does his duty silently and only in his absence do you realize his importance.

All your teachers form the next line of your God on earth.

Your Gurudev, whenever you achieve him, takes control of your life for a significant or the whole of your life. He now becomes the God on the earth.

The cow feeds her milk to you (which was intended for her calf) just like your mother. Your own mother may have fed you for 4, 6, 8 months or a few years, but the cow in some way or the other feeds you throughout your life. That is why, in Sanatana dharma, the cow has been placed at par to your mother, and has been declared as the God on earth. Just as you don't kill your mother when she can't feed you, you shouldn't kill a cow because she is now of no use to you. Killing a cow is akin to killing your mother and is the worst crime in this creation, the punishment for which is only decided by the Lord Himself. Where cows or mothers are killed, there is no hope of righteousness or dharma to be established. Killing a woman is an unpardonable sin as you have killed a mother or would be mother.

The debt that your soul takes in one birth from the mother, cow and the earth/ environment or Prakriti/ your Motherland can never be repaid in a single birth. You must strive hard to serve your mother, the cow and the earth as much as you can, to lessen your debt burden. The more debt you accumulate, it will show in your next birth chart, as retrograde, combust or debilitated planets astrologically and make your life difficult.

The debt from your father, Guru, teachers and other well-wishers can be repaid in this birth.

Try your best not to take unnecessary debts from less known or unknown persons, and take care to pay them off.

Chapter 5:

THE JOURNEY OF THE SOUL

Life is but a journey of the Soul, when an impatient particle of the Universal Energy wants to be free or is commanded to be free. It gets its orders from the Lord to perform its deeds, gets a body, and is sent to one of the worlds. There are 14400 worlds always in this Creation, though not all have lives simultaneously. The Soul starts its journey following the command, and gets its first stoppage in its first life. Often the illusory world deviates it from its original karma and also it accumulates some bad karma in doing misdeeds. Then starts the cycle of its next birth to pay off the accumulated karma, and so on. After many lives, the soul starts realizing that it actually needs to again get reunited with the Lord, and starts to rapidly pay off all pending karmas and races to Moksha, wherein it is again absorbed into the Primordial Energy.

Some evolved souls take birth by the order of the Lord to carry out some specific karma. A detailed study of their birth charts will tell you that. Often you find very good souls, doing very good work, departing quickly. These souls have already fulfilled their purpose and they may be required elsewhere in this world or another, to carry out some other order of the Lord.

Some evil ones don't die quickly. They keep on accumulating bad karmas and suffer diseases, mostly to take a very lowly birth in the next life.

Some persons not really doing great karma still live on, mostly because they still have the potential to do good.

So actually it's a journey of the soul, with sort of stoppages as lives, just like railway stations or bus stoppages. Here you are allotted a specific duty, you select a specific family and your time and Nakshatra of birth to help you in the Prarabdha or destiny, and try to complete the job. In every life, the ultimate objective of the soul is to have been truthful and dutiful throughout your life, you need not be afraid of anything. Always stick to righteousness or Dharma. Dharma is not religion. Religion is a manmade belief system, mostly having some vested interests. Dharma is the true duty of a human being that needs to be done at a certain situation at a certain place and a certain time. Dharma of all human beings facing a particular situation is always the same, whatever his beliefs. If you see someone beating an elderly man, your reaction should always be the same, whoever you are.

If you see a pregnant woman being driven out of her house, your reaction should always be the same regardless of your sex, beliefs, colour of skin or country of origin. This universal call of righteous duty is called Dharma. It's not out of pity. It's something which has been recorded as correct by the Creator.

Whether you look at your watch and walk away, hear a call for prayer and walk away, or do what you should have done as per Dharma is whether you do your proper Karma following your Dharma. This is the concept of Karma following universal Dharma. There is no other karma more important than following the universal dharma. Sometimes the Lord also tests you by presenting you such sudden tests exposing you to a conflicting path. This becomes your karma. Not everything is destined. However, all major events in your life are destined, like your time of birth, your parents, family and place of birth, marriage, child birth, the main duty you have come here to perform and death. These form your Destiny or Prarabdha, over which you have no control.

Chapter 6:

THE KARMAS AND PRARABDHA

Once the body dies, the Atman is free. He has to face a judgement about what his Prarabdha karma was and how far he could achieve. What are his rinas or dues in this life and who all are they that he has been indebted to. What Prarabdha karmas could he not finish and why? What bad karmas did he do? Now he will face the Lord to answer why he did not do what he was sent for, and why he has done for which he cannot face the Lord!

After this assessment, he will be allotted his next birth to any of the four or five worlds which simultaneously always has life. The worst offenders will get lives of vegetation like a tree. He will get a fresh set of Prarabdha from the Lord. Each and every soul has a moral obligation to the Lord to complete his Prarabdha in this life, as it has been ordained by Lord Himself.

Would like to add, we call the Formless One by different names like God, Allah, Mahadeva, Krishna, Buddha etc, but they are names given to the Lord by humans.

Now, having received the orders, the soul searches for a body that will suit this Prarabdha the best. Having chosen the sex, man or woman, the Atman will decide the time, the Lagna, Rashi, Nakshatra, to achieve this Prarabdha the best. Then this part of the Purusha enters the body of a baby or Prakriti, with its first cry at the hour of his choice.

Of course, if the karmas, rinas, incompetence in the previous life regarding the prarabdha is too much, the Atman will not receive a human life.

Having got the desired life and time, now is his turn to come good on his Prarabdha. He has three main things to perform:

1. To always try and know the Formless One

2. To always try to help the Creation by helping others

3. To achieve as close as possible to complete his Prarabdha or Destiny.

In the meanwhile, he has to make sure that he does not pick up bad karmas and not take needless debts from a multitude of people. Try always to clear your debts to as many people as well, rather not take unnecessary ones.

Trying to know God – you require your Guru.

Chapter 7:
HOW TO ACHIEVE YOUR PRARABDHA KARMA?

A true Guru will always know your Prarabdha. Your Ishtadeva, Kuldevata will also help you achieve it. If you know astrology or know a good astrologer he will help you know your Prarabdha. That is why astrology has been called the fifth Veda.

Once you get to roughly know your Prarabdha, put your heart and soul to achieve it. This is the actual reason of your this life. Never blame life for not giving you this and that. To each one of us, the Lord has given us the Soul and mother Nature this body. Now its up to you to do your karma, minimise debts and misdeeds, get a proper Guru and submit completely to the Lord. The rest, you will see, will fall in place. This is the basis of Sanatana or Eternal Dharma. Religion, as we know today, is man made in the last 2000 years, and is eventually of little importance. Always know that you have very little time on this Earth to complete your Prarabdha. The nearer you reach your Prarabdha you will realize there is no time! Don't waste time. Time is your most precious possession in this earth. Don't waste water, food or money. All of us have something unique in excess, be that money, food, resources, knowledge or time. The Lord has given you that excess to distribute among those who are deprived of it.

For example, if you are extra ordinarily intelligent, it is not to be used to cheat and skilfully deceive others, but to help those people who are unintelligent and need help.

Don't fight among yourselves about who is right. Most of the time nobody is! Whenever you are in trouble, get in touch with your Guru. He will always guide you.

It's pathetic and painful to see people fighting over manmade boundaries of this wonderful Creation like Religion, Caste, boundary of a country, colour of skin, while actually the fight should have been between righteousness and unrighteousness (Dharma and Adharma). There will be many who will tell you to fight for a cause, be sure it benefits them somehow. Fight for Righteousness because it benefits the Creation, your future and the future generations.

If you cannot decide what is right, isolate yourself, and ask the question to yourself. Look at Nature, see how the Nature reacts to that question. If possible, discuss with your parents or your Guru.

Chapter 8:

THE CONCEPT OF DAANAM

The Lord asked me in my dream, what do you feel is the best daanam?

Daanam is the giving away of anything which is dear to you wilfully to someone else hence cutting of all mental attachment to it. It is an act rather than Tyaagam which is more inert.

I answered to my Lord, anything which I have in excess.

He smiled and said, that is disposal. You are removing your clutter.

I replied, then its giving something which I have in a small quantity.

He said, the best donation or Daanam is of that which you don't have!

I was confused. How can I donate something which I don't have? It's not mine. Anyway, I went on to sleep. These events happened when I was recovering from an extremely critical illness, adrenal crisis, which got precipitated by a pneumonia I contracted from a patient in 2021, and I was lying in a hospital bed alone, with my dear friend, my Lord as my only companion.

I dreamt that I was heading for an important meeting to New Delhi from Kolkata carrying a briefcase on the Rajdhani express. The meeting was for a critical deal. The train reached somewhere in UP where I alighted to have a cup of tea and have a look around. I found a small boy of about five crying on the platform. I asked him, what has happened. He answered that he has been lost, and cannot find his mother. I tried to look around and ask people. Everyone was too busy to think of the kid. I took him to the station master who told me that he was too busy with important trains now, and that I should consult the Railway Police. I went to the Railway Police station with the boy. They listened to the case, made a report, and told me, Sir, it is our responsibility now and you can leave. The kid clutched on to me, and I told the police, I am going nowhere, and to kindly look for his parents. The police did their job well, and I could see the tears of joy on the face of the boy and the mother on their reunion. I gave them my card, told them they were free to call for any further help. The Police were also very pleased and we shared some sweets and a cup of tea to celebrate a job well done.

By this time, I realized that my train was gone, and I had to reach New Delhi by morning to attend my meeting at 10 am. I asked a taxi to take me to Delhi, and he said, we will make it on time. Sitting in the taxi, I thought why did I donate so much time to an issue which had nothing to do with me, when I had no time at all!

Suddenly I realized that I had just made the supreme daanam! The Lord smiled.

Chapter 9:

THE CONCEPT OF THE SHIVA LINGAM

People often discuss or argue about what really is the Shiva Lingam. Westerners sometimes say it is the symbol of the phallus. Some say it is the model of a molecule, a model of the Nirakara or a pillar of light.

Lord Krishna described the concepts of Prakriti and Purusha to Arjuna and nobody can explain them better. What we can see and feel are all part of Prakriti or the female energy whether it is living or non-living. These are made of Carbon, Oxygen, Nitrogen, trace elements, all of which are found in Nature or our Earth, hence considered as Prakriti. In Sanatani language, Five elements, Air, Water, Fire, Earth and Ether. All of us are made of these elements.

But it is Purusha, the unseen but all-pervading Intellect, which makes us what we are.

This Purusha, the Atman, or the Intellect remains an unseen energy which enters the bundle of Prakriti at the first cry of the baby. Some intellectuals comment that it enters earlier, but I have been told by my Gurudeva that it enters at the contact of the first rays of the Sun, Planets and Nakshatras on the body, which can only be discerned at the first cry of life of the baby which happens soon after.

The mother carries the Prakriti part of the baby in utero for nine months. The Atman having got the orders of Prarabdha karma from the Lord searches for the proper time, planetary positions and Nakshatra to accomplish the Prarabdha. So the basis of Astrology is the urge of the Atman or Purusha to achieve his Prarabdha or destiny by the help of Prakriti or this body.

So when this Intellect or Atman enters this Prakriti, the body becomes a Shiva Lingam. Each and every being on this Creation is a Shiva Lingam or an abstract version of this incredible Creation. This form is neither Akara nor Nirakara, but a very abstract one and only form of this Creation. The Creation or the Lord has been worshipped in this form all over the world since humans existed. Even the birds and animals understand this form. You won't see a bird's droppings or a dog pissing on a Shiva Lingam. Worship of the Lingam is a complete worship of the Creator and His Creation including of the Divine Mother.

Chapter 10:

KEY TAKEAWAYS FOR THE COMMON MAN

This book gives you a philosophical insight to the concepts of God, Creation, Guru and our lives.

The concept of God is purely individualistic and should be kept as such with an open mind.

The choice of ones Guru is an extremely important part of our life. A good Guru can handhold you past the darkest and the most frustrating periods of your life with ease. A Guru is necessary if you seriously mean to enter the spiritual philosophy.

What happens if one does not believe in God or Creation? Well, he misses out on a fascinating facet of life – the spiritual philosophy – one that gives you peace. If peace is your main aim in life, you can never achieve it without this philosophy.

For the common man, it might be too difficult to digest the Vedas, the Geeta, other Holy books, get a proper Guru and understand the difficult philosophy. The easiest thing for them to do is to follow the path of righteousness or Dharma. Follow the path of righteousness, make your living simple, speak the truth, avoid wastage, always be true to yourself and keep a little time for self- evaluation and introspection.

I wish all the readers well in their lives.

I conclude with my regards to my Gurudeva.